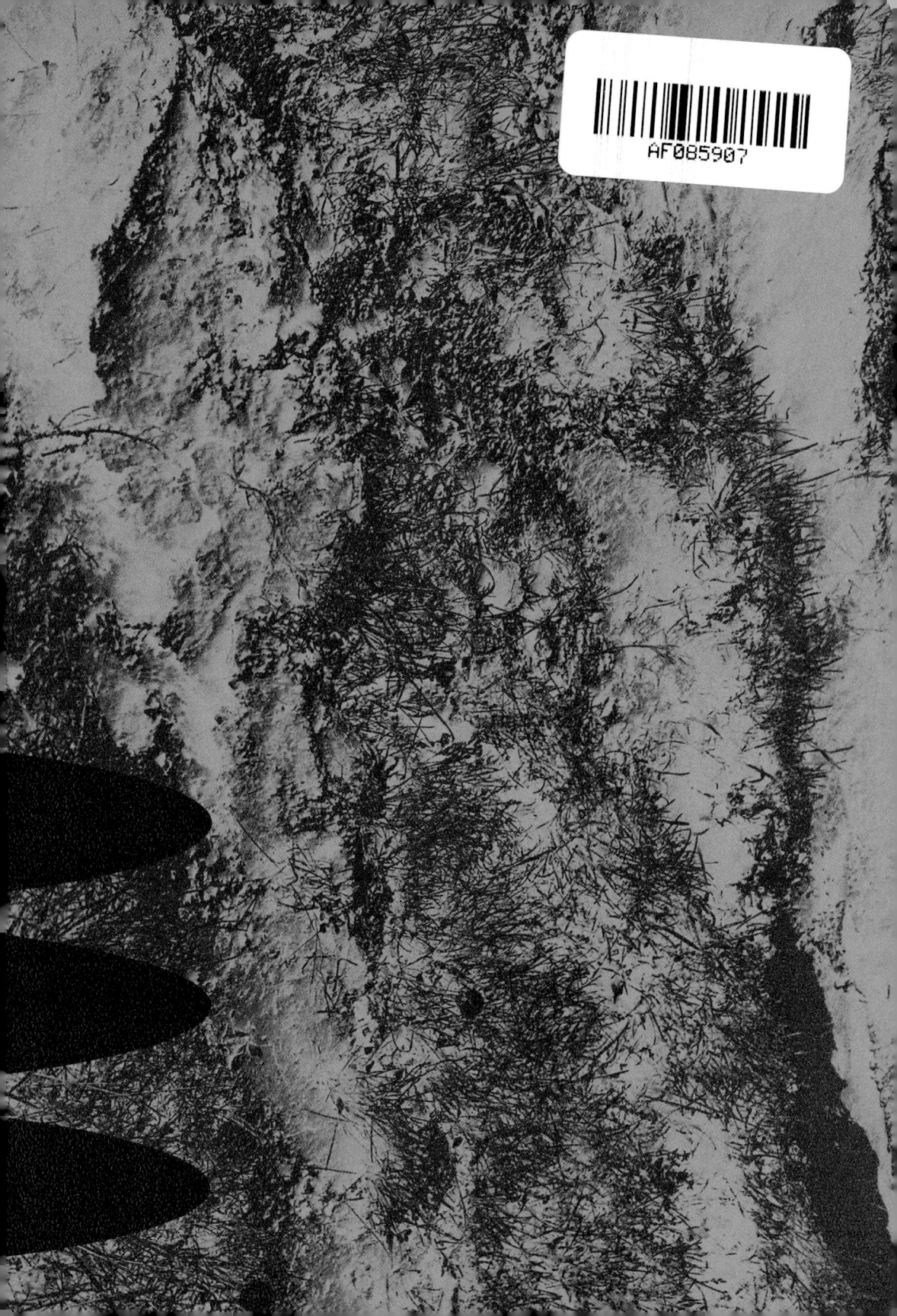

Joel Evey

WE HAVE THE GREAT DISCONTENT

for

Actual Source

04

For over 3 decades, John Shahidi has been dispensing an eclectic mix of printed matter from his unassuming storefront in West Philadelphia.

Stocking publications of every topic and persuasion, Avril 50 is an unexpected delight to those who happen upon it, and for others it's a regular destination to find the printed matter they can't find elsewhere.

Announced to his followers via Avril 50's Facebook page, Shahidi's inventories read like strange run-on poems, their nonsensical syntaxes recalling Dadaist techniques employed to "[free] the unconscious from the domination of reason and tradition."[1]

The following content was posted by Avril 50 between 2014 and 2016.

Gear patrol came with rain system

Bitch is here with hero

Something about man of the world holiday

08

10 men came with another fantastic man

Gentle woman is came with tank

we have

delicious
artichoke

Bespoke

little

white

lies

We got love prospect

We have strip cabinet

man about town
came with damn
teeth system

We have
delicious

pinup

with details

16

We have pinup union

We have elephant at large.

Smith came
with salt
peppermint

Fat hero bitch came

Dazed and
confused

Mark came

put egg on it

She shreds flair

22

We have delicious

mousse

We are getting

sentimental

24

Pop cultured CR came

We got teeth

We got
summerwinter

dinosaur

monrowe
alla carta
plat form

28

Fucking young hero is here

We have calm intercourse

We have Elephant

woman strip

reality show

10 men and 10 women came together

Out of order fool came with citizen K

Monster
children came
with

delay

gratification

34

We got ugly things

Fucking young
hero came
with the great
discontent

disfunkshion
Dave

came today

We got double
peppermint
russh
with man
aboutown

38

Mark came with

bare
hungry
eye

We got fat

Lula is here with out of order lampoon

We got wild

Associated dinosaur elephant is here

We have the great discontent

WE HAVE
THE GREAT
DISCONTENT

Concept:
Joel Evey

Editorial Assistant:
Olivia Verdugo

Printer:
Kopa, LT

Typeface:
Helveestica
By Dinamo

© 2017
Actual Source
& *Joel Evey*

1. Adapted from Pericles Lewis's Cambridge Introduction to Modernism (Cambridge UP, 2007) p. 107.

ISBN: 978-0-9970590-3-8

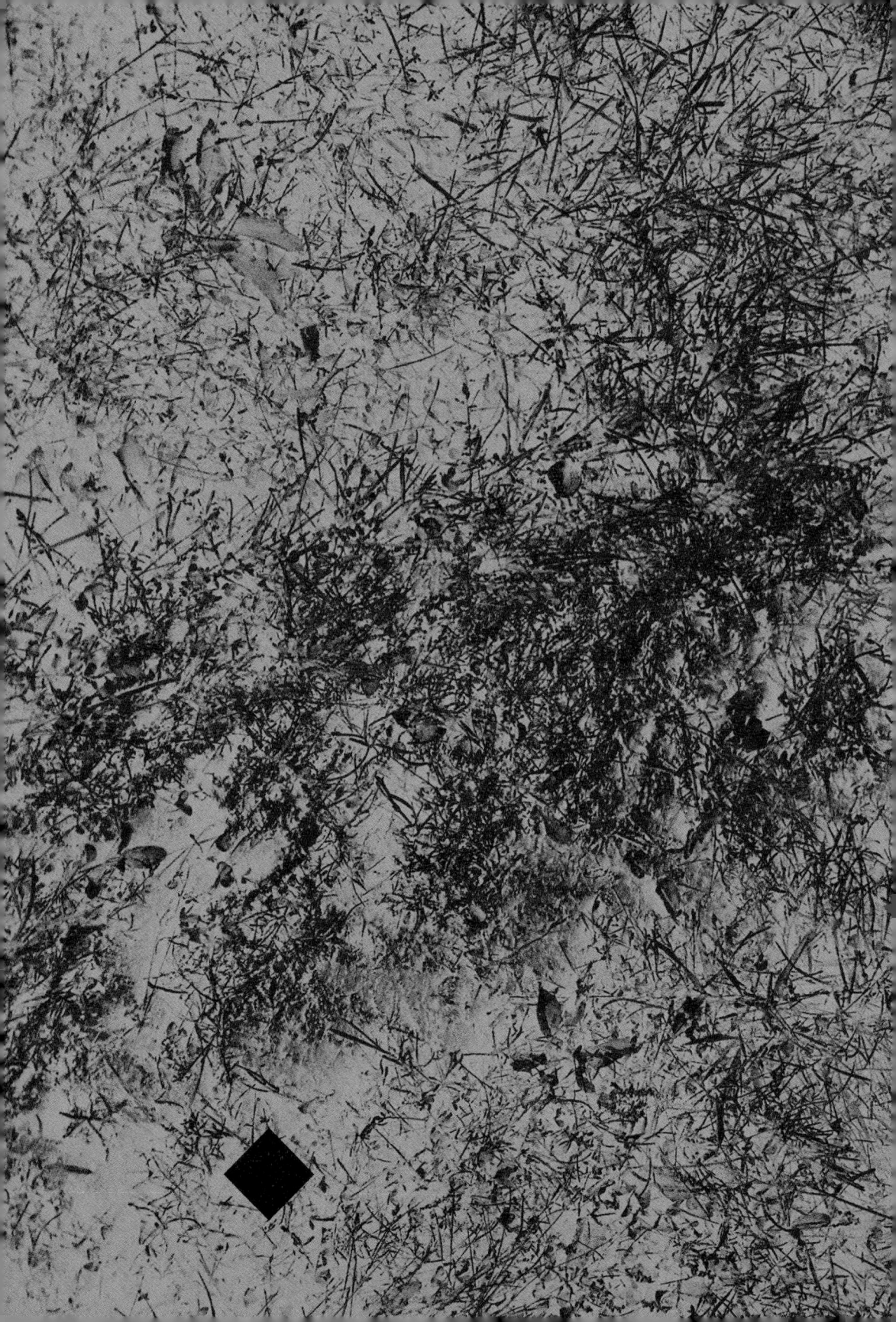